THE BASIS

of

HARMONY

by

FREDERICK J. HORWOOD, Mus. Doc.

Author of "The Basis Of Music"

Copyright U. S. A. 1948 by

GORDON V. THOMPSON LIMITED

TORONTO, CANADA

International Copyright

PRINTED IN CANADA

CONTENTS

CHAPTER I

INTRODUCTION TO HARMONY

Harmony is the art of writing successive chords for voices or instruments in such a way that the music produced is acceptable to the ear. Elementary harmony is the basis of all good music, and should be written for four voices: soprano, alto, tenor and bass.

The student of harmony should know all the major and minor scales with their key signatures; the chromatic scale; also intervals and their inversions. These are all fully discussed in the author's "Basis of Music." (Gordon V. Thompson Limited.)

To make satisfactory progress in harmony, the student should learn to hear what he writes, if he does not already possess that gift. By diligent practice in listening to all musical examples given in the text, he will make considerable progress, although he may not be able to hear four notes together for some time. He will ultimately acquire tonal vision, or ability to hear with the eye, if he will take the time to sing each note within his vocal range, and try to hear the soprano and bass together. Later he may attempt to hear three or four notes at once, and from this stage of progress it is not difficult to listen to complete chords in succession. All experiments with the eye should be checked afterwards at the keyboard.

It should be emphasized that two of the prime essentials in writing harmony are neatness and accuracy. There is a fascination about the writing of music that makes the study of harmony most enjoyable and satisfying. Notes should be carefully decided before they are written down. Speed is not necessary.

Exercises in harmony should never be worked at the keyboard, although the student should play them afterwards to hear the musical result of his work.

The following abbreviations, which have been used in the "Basis of Music" are used throughout this book.

Degrees of the major or minor scales: I. II. III. IV. V. VI. VII.

Intervals: 1. 2. 3. 4. 5. 6. 7. 8. 9.

Qualifying names: (with symbols)

Perfect: P	Major: +	Diminished: 0
	Minor: −	Augmented: ×

Additional abbreviations will be introduced as required.

CHAPTER II

TRIADS IN ROOT POSITION

1. A triad consists of any note with intervals of a third and fifth above it. The note from which a triad is built is called the root. There are four kinds of triads in use:

Major triad: Root, major third and perfect fifth.

Minor triad: Root, minor third and perfect fifth.

Diminished triad: Root, minor third and diminished fifth.

Augmented triad: Root, major third and augmented fifth.

These triads occur on successive notes of any major and minor scale, maintaining the same order as shown in the following examples in C major and C minor. The letter "a" after a Roman numeral indicates that the chord is in root position, that is, with the root in the lowest voice.

The harmonic scale is used at present as the basis of harmony in minor keys.

Ex. 1

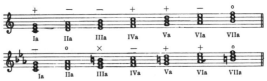

2. If the triads shown above are played on a piano, the major and minor triads sound complete or final. These are classified as common chords, or concords, because they contain consonant intervals only — a perfect fifth with a major or minor third. Diminished and augmented triads sound unfinished or incomplete in themselves, and are known as discords. They do not always sound satisfactory in root position, but when inverted, (root not in the lowest voice) some of them are very useful. Triads that are most effective in root position, therefore, are the concords. There are six of these in major keys, and four in minor:

4

Major keys: Ia. IIa. IIIa. IVa. Va. VIa.
Minor keys: Ia.   IVa. Va. VIa.

The above triads should be checked with the list in **Ex. 1**.

3. *Arranging triads for four voices.*

The range or compass of each voice is as follows:

Ex. 2

Soprano and alto parts use the treble clef, and tenor and bass parts use the bass clef. Stems of soprano and tenor notes should turn upwards, while those of alto and bass should turn downwards. Parts should not cross; that is, the soprano should be the highest note, then the alto, next the tenor, and lowest of all the bass.

Since a triad has only three notes to be divided between four voices, one of the notes must be given to two different voices, either as a unison, or at the distance of one or more octaves. This process is known as doubling. The following rules must be observed in chord construction:

(a) The root of the triad must be in the bass voice.

(b) The third and the fifth may be written in any of the other three voices, and in any order — the third may be placed above or below the fifth, as desired.

(c) In Ia, IVa, and Va, the root should be doubled in the remaining part. In IIa, IIIa, and VIa the root *or* third may be doubled in the remaining part. (Note that IIa and IIIa are not used in minor keys.) *or 5th.*

(d) The alto must not be more than an octave from the soprano or from the tenor, but the tenor may be any reasonable distance from the bass, or may form a unison with it.

Several different arrangements of any triad are possible. Here are some examples which should be checked with the rules given above.

Ex. 3

EXERCISES

Write the following triads for four voices. Each chord should be written in at least five different arrangements.

Aim for neatness and accuracy. Use a ruler for bar lines.

1. Ia   in Keys of D+ . G −, A+, B −, B ♭+ , D −, B+, G ♯− .

2. IIa in Keys of A ♭+ , C ♯− , G+, D ♭+ , E ♭+ , F+ .

3. IIIa in Keys of E +, F ♯+ , G ♭+ , D+, B ♭+ , A+ .

4. IVa in Keys of C −, E ♭+ , A ♭+ , D −, G+, F −, B+, B ♭− .

5. Va   in Keys of F ♯− , G ♯   , D −, B ♭+ , B −, E ♭+ , A ♭+ ,
C ♯+ .

6. VIa in Keys of D −, A −, E −, D ♯− , F ♯+ , D ♭+ , C ♭+ ,
A ♭− .

CHAPTER III

CHORD PROGRESSIONS USING PRIMARY TRIADS

1. A chord progression occurs when two chords are played in succession. A series of chord progressions extending for four bars and ending with a cadence, forms a musical phrase. Two such phrases make a normal sentence or period.

Primary triads are those built upon the three most important degrees of any key: I, IV and V. Since the harmonic scale is the basis for chord progressions in minor keys, (with a few exceptions to be considered later,) the leading note therefore requires an accidental when Va is used in a minor key.

There are only six possible progressions of the primary triads:

Ia — IVa   Ia — Va   IVa — Ia   IVa — Va
Va — IVa   Va — Ia

These progressions may be extended to produce a phrase:

Ia — Va — Ia — IVa — Va — Ia, etc. Chords must be connected grammatically, like words in a sentence; otherwise the music sounds unpleasant.

2. *To join primary triads together*:

(a) A note common to consecutive chords is better retained in the same voice, or part.

(b) Notes which *must* move should proceed the shortest possible distance.

(c) IVa and Va have no note in common. The three upper notes should move in the opposite direction to the bass, and observe rule (b) The leading note in Va should not be in the soprano when IVa and Va are joined.

(d) Sometimes, because of the progression of a given melody, it becomes necessary to omit the fifth from Ia and triple the root. In such a progression the note in common cannot be repeated as suggested in (a).

7

Here are some examples of progressions of primary triads:

Ex. 4

EXERCISES

Aim for neatness and accuracy. Use a ruler for bar lines.

1. Write the following chord progressions in four part harmony in the keys specified:

A + :   Ia — IVa   Va — Ia   IVa — Va   IVa — Ia

B   :   Va — Ia   IVa — Va   Ia — Va   Va — IVa

E♮ + :   IVa — Va — Ia   Va — Ia — IVa   Ia — IVa — Va

G   :   Ia — IVa — Va — Ia   IVa — Va — Ia — Va

       Va — Ia — IVa — Ia

2. Add alto and tenor parts to the following:

3. Add soprano, alto and tenor parts to the following fragments of bass:

CHAPTER IV

CADENCES

1. Cadences are the punctuation marks of music, and create momentary points of pause. A cadence is formed by a specific progression of chords used at the end of a musical phrase. It is possible to produce three types of cadences by means of primary triads:

(a) *Perfect cadence*: also called a full close, or authentic cadence: Va — Ia. This cadence gives a feeling of finality, and is better reserved for the end of a sentence. The tonic is usually the last soprano note, although this is not imperative. Here are some examples of perfect cadences:

Ex. 5

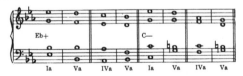

(b) *Imperfect cadence*: or half close: Ia — Va, or IVa — Va. This cadence may be used at the end of any phrase except the last, because it does not end on a tonic chord:

Ex. 6

(c) *Plagal cadence*: or plagal close, or church cadence: IVa—Ia. This may be used at the end of any phrase, but it is frequently found as an addition to a sentence already completed by a perfect cadence. It is also used as the Amen to a hymn tune or anthem:

9

Ex. 7

2. *The Tierce de Picardie*. Sometimes music written in a minor key ends with a major tonic chord. This chord is known as the Tierce de Picardie and is produced by raising the third of Ia by an accidental. It is more commonly used with plagal cadences, but it may also be used in perfect cadences. In any case it must only occur as the final chord of the sentence, and its use is optional:

Ex. 8

3. *Figured bass*. A figured bass is one which contains figures and other signs below the notes to indicate what notes are to be played above. In the time of Handel this type of bass was used extensively for harpsichord accompaniments, the player filling in the missing parts in accordance with the figures below. Such a figured bass was called a "continuo." It is now used only in the study of harmony.

Chords in root position require no figuring unless an accidental occurs in the chord, in which case the same accidental should also appear below the bass note. At present the only accidentals required are those for the third of certain chords in minor keys:

Va requires an accidental to produce the leading note.

Ia requires an accidental when it is used as a Tierce de Picardie.

The following examples show the use of accidentals below the bass:

Ex. 9

4. Extended progressions may now be written, providing the last two chords of a four-bar phrase introduce one of the cadences. The joining of successive chords should present no difficulty. If this series is given: Ia — IVa — Va — Ia; the first two chords should be joined correctly; then Va should be joined to IVa, and lastly Ia joined to the preceding Va:

Ex 10

EXERCISES

Aim for *neatness* and *accuracy*.

1. Write the following cadences:
   (a) Perfect in E♭+ , F♯− , B+ , D− , G.♭+ .
   (b) Two forms of Imperfect in G+ , E+ , F− , B− , A♭+ .
   (c) Plagal in A+ , E− , B♭+ , G− , F♯+ .
   (d) Plagal with Tierce de Picardie in B− , A− , C♯− , E♭− , G♯− .

2. Add three parts above each of the following fragments of bass.

CHAPTER V

SECONDARY TRIADS

1. The available secondary triads are IIa, IIIa, VIa in major keys, and VIa in minor keys.

These· triads are helpful in avoiding monotony which would otherwise occur from the excessive use of primary triads. Secondary triads of the major key are closely related to the primary triads, occurring as they do on the notes of their relative minor scales:

Ex. 11

Each of the secondary triads has its own special use as follows:

(a) *IIa in major keys*. This is a minor triad, and the root or the third may be doubled. It forms an imperfect cadence when followed by Va. It makes an excellent approach to a perfect cadence: IIa — Va — Ia. When followed ·by Va, it is better if the note common to both chords is *not* kept in the same part. Except in the bass, the notes should move as smoothly as possible:

Ex. 12

3rd doubled

(b) *IIIa in major keys*. This chord is less frequently used than the other secondary triads because it is indefinite: the lower part of the triad is also part of the tonic chord, while the upper part suggests the dominant chord. The root or third may be doubled. It is better reserved for use as follows: Preceded or followed by Ia or VIa; or followed by IVa, if the leading note in IIIa is written in the soprano as part of a descending scale passage:

Ex. 13

(c) *VIa in major or minor keys.* This chord may be used on any occasion as a substitute for Ia. When preceded by Va it produces a new cadence: *Deceptive cadence* — false close, or interrupted cadence: Va — VIa. In this progression the bass rises one step; the leading note rises one step; and the other two notes fall. The result it that the third of VIa is doubled. This is imperative in minor keys, but in the major key the root of VIa may be doubled occasionally:

Ex. 14

root doubled

The deceptive cadence is useful in avoiding a full close at the end of a phrase. If VIa moves to Va, another form of the imperfect cadence is produced. It is now possible to write four forms of the imperfect cadence in major keys and three forms in minor keys:

Major keys: Ia — Va. IIa — Va. IVa — Va. VIa — Va.
Minor keys: Ia — Va.   IVa — Va. VIa — Va.

Ex. 15

2. The musical effect of a chord progression depends chiefly on the movement of the root. The following table of root progressions should be memorized:

(a) Roots moving a fourth or a fifth are excellent.

(b) Roots rising a third are weak, but are not objectionable within a bar — from an accented beat to an unaccented beat.

(c) Roots falling a third are good, but not so strong as those moving a fourth.

(d) Roots rising a second are good except IIa to IIIa.

13

(e) Roots falling a second are bad, except VIa to Va, and Va to IVa (providing the leading note is *not* in the soprano).

3. *How to join any two chords together*:

(a) Roots moving a fourth or fifth:

Let the note common to both chords be retained in the same voice, except in IIa to Va. The other two notes should move as smoothly as possible.

Ex. 16

(b) Roots moving a third:

Let the two notes in common be retained in the same voice. The third note should move by step in the opposite direction (contrary motion) to the bass.

Ex. 17

(c) Roots moving a second:

In Ia — IIa and IVa — Va, the three upper voices should move in contrary motion to the bass. In Va — VIa, and VIa — Va, two voices should move up and two down. The leading note should rise in Va — VIa, and the third of VIa should be doubled.

Ex. 18

14

4. *Forbidden progressions of parts.*

If the preceding rules are observed, the following mistakes should not occur, but since in more advanced work there will be the temptation to move in the wrong direction, these common errors and prohibitions are listed:

(a) A part should not proceed by an augmented interval (× 2, × 4, × 5); but a diminished interval is good if it is approached from and left by notes *within* that interval:

Ex. 19

(b) Two adjacent parts must not overlap; for example, the alto of one chord should not move to a higher note than the soprano of the preceding chord, nor should the bass move to a higher note than the preceding tenor note. An exception to this rule is permitted when two different positions of the same chord are used in succession:

Ex. 20

(c) The leap of a major seventh is not good. The leap of a minor seventh is permitted if procedure is observed similar to that governing the leap of a diminished fifth.

Ex. 21

(d) The leading note usually rises, except in a descending scale passage. It may fall to the dominant if the progression is in the alto or tenor voice.

15

Ex. 22

good   good   good   not good

(e) *N.B.* No two parts are allowed to move by consecutive octaves or by consecutive fifths:

Ex. 23

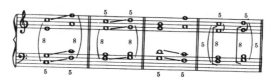

(f) The soprano and bass must not approach an octave or fifth by similar motion (both parts moving in the same direction) except under the following conditions:

1. If the soprano moves by step and one or both chords are primary triads;

2. If the soprano leaps, and two positions of the same chord are used in succession;

3. If the chords are IIa — Va, the soprano may approach a fifth by similar motion, leaping down a third:

Any other form of approach to such intervals produces what is known as exposed octaves or fifths.

Ex. 24

Va   Ia   IVa   Ia   Ia   Va   IIa   Va

5. *Cadential approaches.* The chord preceding any cadence should be a different chord from either of those used in the cadence: IIa — Va — Ia, etc. The chord of approach to a perfect cadence may also be IVa or VIa. An apparent exception to the rule is that Ia may

precede IVa, when a plagal cadence is used as an extension to a phrase or sentence:

Ex. 25

not good   good   good

EXERCISES

Aim for *neatness* and *accuracy*.

1. Write four different imperfect cadences in each of these keys: G+, D♭+, B+, E+.

2. Write three different imperfect cadences in each of these keys: E−, C♯−, G−, B−, F−.

3. Write a deceptive cadence in each of these keys: E+, A+, G♭+, C♯−, F♯−, B♭−.

4. Add three parts above these fragments of bass:

CHAPTER VI

FIRST INVERSIONS OF TRIADS

1. The first inversion of any triad is formed by placing the third of the chord in the bass. This arrangement of notes produces intervals of a third and a sixth above the bass, and the chord is sometimes called a six-three chord, or chord of the sixth.

A chord of the sixth may be formed on any note of the major scale. Such chords are symbolized by the Roman numeral of the degree of the scale on which the root falls, followed by the letter "b."

The following first inversions occur in major keys:

Ex. 26

In minor keys, the chord IIIb is seldom used and should be avoided in elementary work. This leaves six first inversions in minor keys:

Ex. 27

The figure 6 is used below bass notes when first inversions are required. This figure is an abbreviation for $\frac{6}{3}$, the intervals found above the bass. In minor keys the 6 must be preceded by an accidental when VIIb is used, to indicate the accidental for the leading note which is now a sixth above the bass:

18

Ex. 28

2. *Doubling of notes in first inversions*:

Any note of a first inversion *may* be doubled, except the leading note, but it is helpful to follow these suggestions concerning the best note to double:

(a) In Ib, IVb, and Vb, double the root, which is now the 6th above the bass.

(b) In the other first inversions double the bass, which is the third of the chord. Here are some good arrangements of first inversions of triads, following the above recommendations:

Ex. 29

The sixth from the bass is usually the best soprano note, if a choice is offered. When writing harmony with a mixture of root positions and first inversions, this is a good plan:

If the root is in the bass, write the third in the soprano.

If the third is in the bass, write the root in the soprano.

There are occasions where this cannot be done, but such exceptions will cause the student little trouble, if he adopts the above as a general rule.

Ex. 30

3. *The use of VIIb.* This chord contains a diminished fifth from the root, which is a dissonant interval, and requires special treatment. It is most effective when used between Ia and Ib, or Ib and Ia, so that the progression is Ia — VIIb — Ib, or the same chords in reverse order. This idiom of three chords occurs very frequently at the beginning of phrases. It should be memorized, and used whenever the given melody or bass permits. In the following examples all parts move smoothly. In the first and second examples, there are consecutive fifths between the alto and tenor, but since one of the fifths is diminished, they are not objectionable.

Ex. 31

A perfect and diminished fifth may follow each other in either order if the lower part concerned moves a *semitone* and if the bass voice is not involved.

Ex. 32

VIIb may also be joined to VIb, or VIa, but it should never move to Va, as the progression sounds weak:

Ex. 33

4. *Successive chords of the sixth.* It is difficult and not always effective to join chords in root position when the roots move a second. This difficulty vanishes when the chords are in first inversion. A

20

series of two or more first inversions over a bass that moves by step is good. In such progressions it is helpful to follow these rules:

(a) The sixth above the bass should be in the soprano.

(b) The third above the bass should be in the alto.

(c) The tenor should double the third and sixth alternately, avoiding the doubled leading note.

This treatment of the chords prevents consecutive fifths and octaves:

Ex. 34

5. *Other uses of first inversions.*

(a) IIb, like IIa makes a good approach to Va and is therefore an excellent precadential chord to an imperfect, perfect, or deceptive cadence. It is also available in a minor key, whereas IIa is prohibited:

Ex. 35

(b) VIb lacks character in the major key but is excellent in the minor key. It is usually connected to Vb or VIIb, also to Ia:

Ex. 36

(c) One of the two chords forming a perfect or imperfect cadence may be inverted, but in plagal and deceptive cadences both chords are better in root position:

Ex. 37

(d) In figuring a bass, first inversions are best used when the bass moves by step. If the bass leaps a fourth or fifth, both chords are better in root position. In working a figured bass, the soprano should be added first if possible, with due respect to the rule that when the root is in one part the third should be in the other. Afterwards the alto and tenor parts should be filled in. It is not necessary, and often not possible to make these inner parts very interesting with the present limited harmonic resources. Here is a figured bass with the upper parts added according to the suggestions given:

Ex. 38

6. *The leading note in minor keys.*

So many grammatical errors occur in the minor key because the leading note is not respected, that the following rules are given in order to prevent errors which so commonly occur in elementary work. It should be remembered that the harmonic form of the scale is the basis of harmony in minor keys.

The leading note:

(a) Must not be doubled.

(b) Must have an accidental.

(c) Should be preceded in the same part by a higher note.

(d) Should rise in the same part to the nearest available note, unless the chord of which it forms a part is followed by another position of the same chord.

(e) In the soprano may be harmonized by Va or VIIb.

(f) In the bass should be figured 6, as it must be part of Vb.

Notice in the following example that the movement of the leading note conforms to the rules given above:

Ex. 39

EXERCISES

Aim for *neatness* and *accuracy*.

1. Write two arrangements of each of the following chords:

Ib   in D + , B − , G − , A + , F − .

IIb   in F ♯− , C ♯− , B ♭+ , A ♭+ , G + .

IIIb in F + , B ♭+ , A + F ♯+ .

IVb   in D − , G ♯− , B ♭− , B + , A ♭+ .

Vb   in E + , E ♭− , C ♯− , D + , A + .

VIb   in A − , D − , F − , D ♭+ , B ♭− .

VIIb in E − , G ♯− , G − , E ♭+ , F + .

2. Write the idiom Ia — VIIb — Ib in D ♭+ , F − , E + , C − .
3. Write the idiom Ib — VIIb — Ia in A ♭+ , C −, F − , B + .
4. Write the progression IIb — Va — Ia in E + , A + , G − , D − .
5. Add three parts above the following figured basses:

23

CHAPTER VII

HARMONIZATION OF MELODIES

1. The harmonization of melodies has been delayed until the student has had experience in writing root positions and first inversions of triads above a given bass. Now that chord progressions have been learned, the adding of three parts below a given melody may be attempted. The available chords already discussed may now be listed:

Major keys:	Ia	IIa	IIIa	IVa	Va	VIa	
	Ib	IIb	IIIb	IVb	Vb	VIb	VIIb
Minor keys:	Ia			IVa	Va	VIa	
	Ib	IIb		IVb	Vb	VIb	VIIb

The following suggestions should be followed carefully:

(a) Write the bass of the cadence to be used at the end of each phrase. The final cadence is usually perfect, but occasionally plagal. (When the second chord of any cadence falls on the weak beat of the bar, the phrase is said to have a feminine ending.)

(b) Write the bass of the precadential chords, using IIa or IIb where possible. If these chords do not fit, use IVa or VIa, or even Ib.

(c) Complete the bass, keeping in mind the using of a reasonable number of first inversions. Remember that a soprano note may be the root, third, or fifth of a chord, and each chord may be in root position or first inversion, so that theoretically there are six possible chords available, although this number is sometimes reduced because of the prohibited chords: IIa, IIIa, VIIa and IIIb in minor keys, and VIIa in major keys.

(d) Try to use the idiom Ia — VIIb — Ib or the reverse when possible, at the beginning of a phrase.

(e) Do not repeat a chord over the bar-line, except at the beginning of a phrase. A chord may at any time be repeated inside a bar, although a change of harmony is stronger.

(f) Try to write the root of the chord in the bass when the third is in the melody, and vice versa. Aim for contrary motion to the soprano when possible, but if bass and treble move by similar motion, a series of first inversions is good.

24

(g) Fill in the middle parts, avoiding consecutive fifths and octaves, etc.

Ex. 40

2. *Sequences.* A sequence is the repetition of a melodic or harmonic progression at another pitch. This device is always good and gives unity to a composition. The simplest method of producing a harmonic sequence is to use a series of chords with roots rising a fourth and falling a fifth alternately. This is sometimes known as the dominant sequence. Here is the bass of such a sequence:

Ex. 41

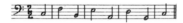

If the first progression in a sequential passage is written correctly, the same pattern may be reproduced above each successive pair of chords. Not more than three statements of a sequential pattern should be used, or the music will become monotonous. The sequential bass given above is now harmonized with chords in root position. It will be observed that VIIa is used, and the leading note doubled. Such a license is allowed in a sequence, provided the first statement of the pattern is correct:

Ex. 42

It is not necessary that all the chords of the dominant sequence be in root position, nor is it imperative that a sequence should be written with roots moving a fourth and fifth, although these are strongest and most effective. Here is a sequence with the same root progressions as those in the preceding example, but with alternate chords in first inversion. The leading note is doubled in the third chord to preserve the sequential pattern:

Ex. 43

3. *The melodic minor scale.* Occasionally a composer wishes to use the melodic minor scale to avoid the interval of an augmented second between VI and VII of the scale, which was originally considered difficult to sing.

When the melodic minor scale is used in any voice, that part should proceed according to one of the followings patterns. The characteristic notes of the melodic scale are marked   :

Ex. 44

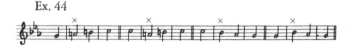

In ascending passages the raised submediant (+ VI) of the scale is used. In descending passages the lowered leading note (– VII) of the scale is used. In both cases the movement of an augmented second is avoided. These two notes cause new triads to be available in minor keys:

+VI may be harmonized by IIa, IIb, IVa and IVb

–VII may be harmonized by IIIa, IIIb, Va, Vb, VIIa and VIIb:

Ex. 45

It should be remembered that IIa, IIIa, IIIb and VIIa are only used when harmonizing + VI and − VII of the melodic minor scale, because they are all concords. In the harmonic scale they are all discords and are prohibited.

When these chords are in root position, the root is the best note to double in the major chords (IIIa, IVa and VIIa). The third or the root may be doubled in the minor chords (IIa and Va). Any note may be doubled in the first inversions except VI.

In descending scale passages, the last chord of the four used for the melodic scale pattern should be the true dominant chord with the leading note raised, so that the minor key may be definitely established.

Ex. 46

Two notes of a melody may frequently be harmonized by one chord, especially when such notes are a fourth apart.

EXERCISES

Aim for *neatness* and *accuracy*.
Harmonize the following melodies adding three parts.

27

- M E M O -

CHAPTER VIII

PASSING NOTES

1. Passing notes are those which do not belong to the chord being used, but are inserted as connecting links between chords. They are also called unessential notes, and for the present should be used only on the weak part of the beat or on unaccented beats. They are more effective in the soprano than in any other voice, although they may be used in any part, or even in two parts at once. The following rules govern the insertion of passing notes:

(a) A passing note must be approached and left by step, moving in scalewise manner; therefore the interval of a third between two harmony notes may be conveniently filled in if no grammatical errors, (which will presently be listed), occur. Two successive passing notes may be used between the fifth and the root of chords Ia, Ib, and IVa and IVb:

Ex. 47

(b) The subdominant of the key as a passing note sounds harsh if the mediant is heard below it:

Ex. 48

(c) Passing notes must not be used if they produce consecutive fifths:

Ex. 49

(d) Passing notes between consecutive fifths or octaves do not destroy the effect of the consecutives. A passage incorrect without them is equally incorrect with them:

Ex. 50

(e) Congestion of parts should be avoided. This is caused in one of two ways: by moving into a unison by step (known as oblique motion); and by leaving a second by similar motion:

Ex. 51

(f) Passing notes may occur in two parts at once (but never more than two) under these conditions: If the two parts move in parallel thirds or sixths, or if the two parts move through an octave by contrary motion:

Ex. 52

2. *Additional rules for minor keys*:

(a) The harmonic scale should be used for chord construction.

(b) The interval of an augmented second must be avoided, by altering the passing note either by inserting or omitting an accidental. This may cause some peculiar irregularities, for example:— in an ascending scale passage it may become necessary to omit the accidentals, and to insert them in a descending passage, thus apparently contradicting the melodic scale:

Ex. 53

In the example above it is necessary to use A flat in the soprano because it is a note of the chord which belongs to the harmonic scale. To avoid the augmented second, it becomes necessary to use B flat as a passing note. Similarly in the second example, B natural occurs in the soprano because it is a note of the chord. To avoid the augmented second, A natural must be used as the passing note. There are of course many cases where the ascending and descending forms of the scale occur in the ordinary way, but the principle is the same; use the harmonic scale for chord construction, and adjust the passing notes to avoid an augmented second.

When two passing notes are used in succession over Ia or Ib, both passing notes are raised in ascending passages and lowered when descending:

Ex. 54

3. *Figuring of passing notes.*

Passing notes are not always indicated in a figured bass and are frequently inserted at the will of the composer, but if specific passing

31

notes are required, the following list may serve as a guide:

8 7   The root of the chord is doubled and moves downwards
      through a passing note.

6 5   The sixth from the bass in a first inversion moves down-
      wards through a passing note.

5 6   The fifth from the bass of a triad moves upwards through
      a passing note.

3 4   The third from the bass moves upwards through a passing
      note.

3 2   The third from the bass moves downwards through a pass-
      ing note.

———— A dash under a bass note indicates that the upper parts
      remain constant while the bass voice moves. Even under
      these conditions the bass need not be a passing note, but
      may be another note of the same chord. When a dash is
      preceded by a figure, the note or notes represented by that
      figure are held while the other parts move.

Remember, that figures refer to distances above the bass, never
to the particular part in which the notes occur.

Ex. 55

EXERCISES

Aim for *neatness* and *accuracy*.

1. Re-write the following, inserting passing notes in any parts
where appropriate:

32

2. Add three parts above each of these figured basses:

3. Harmonize these melodies in four parts, treating unaccented eighth notes as passing notes:

CHAPTER IX

TWO AND THREE PART HARMONY

1. *Two-part harmony.* The student has now learned how to make use of triads and their first inversions, with passing notes. This technique may be used for adding a melody above a bass, or a bass below the melody, with each part of equal interest, and with the chords defined in such a way that alto and tenor are not required.

Since it takes three notes to make a chord, it is not strictly correct to speak of harmony in two parts, but the term is used for the sake of convenience. When a melody and bass are combined in an interesting way the result is known as counterpoint. The following suggestions show how to accomplish this:

(a) With the exception of the first and last notes of an exercise, every harmony note should have a third or a sixth to accompany it and thus define the chord. A fifth or an octave may be used occasionally if approached by contrary motion.

(b) Not more than four consecutive sixths or thirds should be used, or there will be too much similar motion.

(c) The cadences must be clearly defined at the end of each phrase; the first phrase ends with an imperfect or deceptive cadence, and the final cadence is usually perfect.

(d) After the harmony notes have been written, a few passing notes should be inserted in accordance with the rules of the previous chapter.

(e) The rhythm of the two parts should be varied, so that when short notes are being used in one part the other part will have longer notes.

(f) Both parts should be reasonably close together, since there is no alto or tenor.

Here is a melody of eight bars with a skeleton bass written and symbolized:

Ex. 56

The example is now re-written with the addition of passing notes:

Ex. 57

No additional difficulty occurs if the bass is given and the soprano is added above it. The rules given above also apply to this type of exercise.

2. *Three-part harmony.* Three part harmony is better when written for soprano, alto and bass. The soprano and bass are written as in two-part work, and the alto is added afterwards to complete the chords. The following suggestions should be helpful:—

(a) Chords are better completed if possible, although it is not always convenient to write three different notes in a chord. The fifth, or even the root of a chord may be omitted, but never the third. Any note except the leading note may be doubled in an incomplete chord, but unless contrary motion is employed, the major third is better not doubled if another note is available for that purpose.

(b) Interest may be maintained by breaking a chord into shorter notes on the unaccented beats.

The following example shows how three-part harmony appears when worked correctly. Either the soprano or bass may be considered as the given part:

Ex. 58

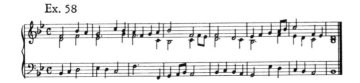

When the soprano is given the bass should be added first, then the alto; but if the bass is given, (i) the soprano may be added first, then the alto, or (ii) both upper parts may be written together.

The soprano and alto parts are also better if kept reasonably close together.

EXERCISES

Aim for *neatness* and *accuracy*.

1. Add a bass to each of the following melodies:

2. Add a soprano above each of the following basses:

3. Add a soprano and an alto above the following figured basses:

4. Harmonize the following melody in three parts, adding bass and alto:

CHAPTER X

SECOND INVERSIONS OF TRIADS

Second inversions of triads are known as six-four chords, because intervals of a sixth and fourth occur above the bass note. The figuring is $\frac{6}{4}$ for which there is no abbreviation. Here are the chords of C major and A minor with their inversions and the complete figuring:

Ex. 59

Six-four chords may be symbolized by the use of the letter "c" after the Roman numeral for the root, such as Ic, IVc, Vc.

These chords require special treatment, and must be followed in a certain way to satisfy the ear, since the fourth from the bass is somewhat discordant.

The student is advised to use only the $\frac{6}{4}$ chords with roots I, IV and V.

The bass of a six-four chord should always be doubled.

There are five different uses of the six-four which are now listed, with rules for the correct treatment of each:

1. *Cadential six-four.* As its name implies, it is used in cadences.

   (a) It should be built on the dominant when used in imperfect, perfect and deceptive cadences. When used in a plagal cadence it is built on the tonic. — *Appogiatura*

   (b) It should move to a triad in root position on the same bass note.

   (c) If it occurs on the dominant it must not be preceded by a chord containing the leading note.

   (d) The figuring also includes that of the chord which follows it: $\frac{6}{4}$ $\frac{5}{3}$ The sixth of the $\frac{6}{4}$ chord usually proceeds to the fifth of the $\frac{5}{3}$ and the fourth falls to the third. The bass is doubled in both chords, and may be repeated, or held; or it may move an octave.

Here are cadential six-fours used in each of the four cadences:

Ex. 60

2. *Passing six-four.* This chord passes from one chord to another, and is better used only between Ia and Ib, Ib and Ia, IVa and IVb, IVb and IVa.

(a) The passing six-four should be built on a passing bass note between the chords mentioned above.

(b) All parts should move as smoothly as possible, and it is better that the six-four occur on the unaccented beat.

(c) It may be used at the beginning of any phrase as an alternative to VIIb between Ia and Ib:

Ex. 61

3. *Auxiliary six-four.* This is also called a pedal six-four, because the bass remains stationary, and such a bass note is known as a pedal note. This six-four occurs only between two statements of Ia or Va. The fourth should be preceded and followed by the third, and the sixth should have a fifth before and after it, while the bass is doubled. The three chords require this figuring

Ex. 62

When the auxiliary six-four occurs at the end of a sentence following a perfect cadence it produces a plagal extension (Ia — IVc — Ia). In such cases the bass should be doubled by the soprano. In the preceding Va chord the leading note is permitted to fall to the dominant in a middle voice in order to make Ia complete:

Ex. 63

4. *Arpeggio six-four*. This chord usually occurs on the weak beat.
   (a) It must be preceded by another position of the same chord; for example, Ic must be preceded by Ia or Ib.
   (b) It must be followed by:
       Another position of the same chord, or
       Any chord on the bass note one step above or below the bass of the six-four:

Ex. 64

5. *Appoggiatura six-four*. This chord is really a passing six-four preceded by Ib and followed by a cadential six-four over the tonic bass. The bass therefore always moves III, II, I, and the pattern given in this example should be reproduced in any required key:

Ex. 65

6. *Suggestions for the use of six-four chords:*

(a) If a cadence permits the use of a six-four chord, it is always good to use it.

(b) A long dominant note in the bass at the end of any phrase suggests a cadential six-four, followed by a $\frac{5}{3}$ on the same bass note.

(c) If a melody begins with III, II, I, a passing six-four is suggested. If it ends with these notes, use a cadential six-four.

(d) If the bass or melody opens with a long note — tonic or dominant, use an auxiliary six-four.

(e) If the last bass note is extended, a plagal extension should be used.

Finally it should be said that, whereas a cadential six-four strengthens a cadence, and a plagal extension (auxiliary six-four) makes a good close, other types of six-four should be used sparingly.

Here is a passage containing various kinds of six-four chords:

Ex. 66

EXERCISES

Aim for *neatness* and *accuracy*.

1. Write one example of each type of six-four chord in each of the following keys:

(The correct preceding and succeeding chords should be used.)
A +, B −, D ♭+ , G −, E ♭+ , E −, F ♯− , B ♭−

2. Add three parts above each of the following figured basses:

41

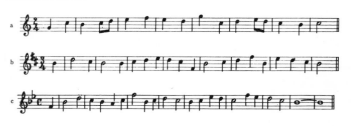

3. Harmonize these melodies, using six-four chords where convenient to do so:

CHAPTER XI

DOMINANT SEVENTH CHORDS

1. The dominant seventh chord is formed by adding another third above the chord Va in major or minor keys. This additional third is now the minor seventh above the root, and thus the chord is named dominant seventh. The intervals above the root are major third, perfect fifth and minor seventh, and the chord is identical in both the major and minor keys, although the third of the chord requires an accidental in the minor key:

Ex. 67

There are three inversions of the dominant seventh, since the chord contains four different notes, each one of which in turn may become the bass. The symbols for the dominant seventh and its inversions are V7a, V7b, V7c, V7d·

Ex. 68

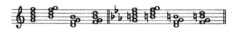

2. *Resolutions of the dominant seventh.* The seventh is a discord and requires resolution — that is, the discordant note must move in a prescribed way to satisfy the ear. The resolution is usually produced by the seventh falling one step to the next note of the scale.

(a) V7a may be resolved in three ways: on Ia, its *normal* or natural resolution, forming a perfect cadence when the bass moves to the tonic, the seventh and fifth fall, and the third rises. The chord of resolution has no fifth, and the root is tripled. If it is desired to complete Ia, omit the fifth of V7 and double the root. Occasionally both chords are complete, but only when the leading note is in the alto or the tenor is it allowed to fall:

Ex. 69

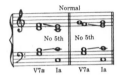

V7a may resolve on VIa, and this is known as the *deceptive* resolution. The bass moves up one step and the other notes move as in the preceding resolution. A deceptive cadence is thus formed. Another resolution of V7a, rarely used, is the *stationary* resolution to IVb, with the seventh remaining stationary:

Ex. 70

(b) V7b has only one resolution — to Ia. The seventh and fifth fall, the third rises, and the root, being common to both chords, is repeated:

Ex. 71

(c) There are two resolutions of V7c:

Its *normal* resolution to Ia, with the seventh and fifth falling and third rising.

Its *exceptional*, or rising resolution, or upward resolution to Ib. In this case the root is repeated and the other three notes all rise one step. This resolution is most important and musically it is very effective:

Ex. 72

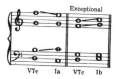

(d) V7d has only one resolution — to Ib, with the seventh and fifth falling and the third rising:

Ex. 73

3. *Ornamental resolutions.* Any of the resolutions discussed may become ornamental by allowing the seventh to move to another note of the chord before resolving:

Ex. 74

4. *Figuring of dominant sevenths.* The following figures indicate the notes of the dominant seventh and its inversions above the given bass:

V7a	7 5 3	V7b	6 5 3	V7c	6 4 3	V7d	6 4 2

Abbreviations:

	7 or 7 3		6 5		4 3		4 2

Complete figuring is sometimes required in minor keys, when certain notes need accidentals. These must be shown in the figures:

Ex. 75

Dominant sevenths in perfect or deceptive cadences may be preceded by a cadential six-four. A dominant seventh must not be used as the second chord of an imperfect cadence. The third inversion of V7 may follow acceptably a cadential six-four (Ic — V7d). Here is a chart to assist the student to remember the resolutions of the dominant seventh:

Ex. 76

A CONDENSED CHART FOR TREATMENT OF V7 CHORDS

Position	Symbol	Figuring	Abbreviation	Resolution	Remarks
Root	V7a	7 5 3	7 or 7 3	Ia VIa IVb	7 falls. 3 rises 5 omitted from one chord 7 falls. 3 rises 7 stationary
1st inversion	V7b	6 5 3	6 5	Ia	7 falls. 3 rises
2nd inversion	V7c	6 4 3	4 3	Ia Ib	7 falls. 3 rises 7 rises. 3 rises
3rd inversion	V7d	6 4 2	4 2	Ib	7 falls. 3 rises

EXERCISES

Aim for *neatness* and *accuracy*.

1. Write and resolve the dominant seventh and inversions with its normal resolutions in G+, B−, A♭+, F−, C♯−, D♭+, G♯−.

2. Write the dominant seventh and inversions with normal resolutions using D as the *bass note* of each chord. Resolve each one in a major key.

3. Write a similar exercise to the above using B as the bass note for each chord, and resolve each one in a minor key.

4. Write the deceptive resolution of V7a in A−, G+, B♭+, F♯−, D−, E+.

5. Write the exceptional resolution of V7c, in D+, B+, A♭+, F−, B♭−', A♭−.

6. Write the stationary resolution of V7a in G♭+, F+, E−, D.♯.

7. Write an ornamental resolution of the dominant seventh and its inversions in F+, A+, E♭−, C−.

8. Add three parts above the following basses:

9. Harmonize the following melodies, using several dominant sevenths or inversions:

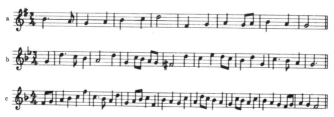

47

CHAPTER XII

OTHER UNESSENTIAL NOTES

1. *Unaccented auxiliary notes.*

These may be written between two statements of the same harmony note in any voice, or in any two voices simultaneously. They must be approached and left by step, returning to the note which preceded. They are really upper or lower decorative notes.

(a) Upper auxiliary notes are better used in the soprano, or in soprano and alto together.

(b) Lower auxiliary notes are always good when used a semitone below the harmony notes, and in some cases an accidental is required to produce the semitone. If the lower auxiliary note is a tone below, it should belong to the key suggested by the chord. Here are some examples. In the fourth of these the auxiliary note F is not good because it is not in the key of G, which is suggested by the chord of G. F sharp would be correct:

Ex. 77

(c) Two upper or lower auxiliary notes may be used in parallel thirds or sixths only. If one of the lower auxiliary notes requires an accidental, the other should be approached by a semitone. Since upper auxiliary notes require no accidentals, they follow the diatonic scale when used in pairs:

Ex. 78

2. *Appoggiaturas.* An appoggiatura is an unessential note used on an accented beat, thus displacing one of the notes of the chord and creating a discord, which resolves at once into a concord. There are four ways of approaching an appoggiatura, but it must always proceed by step, either up or down, usually the latter:

(a) By step in the same direction as that in which it is to move, thus becoming an accented passing note. The note displaced by such passing note or appoggiatura is better not doubled, except in the bass:

Ex. 79

(b) By step from the opposite direction — becoming an accented auxiliary note. The note displaced should not be doubled, except in the bass:

Ex. 80

(c) By leap from any note, usually from the opposite direction to the subsequent movement of the appoggiatura. Any leap to the appoggiatura — augmented or diminished, is allowed:

Ex. 81

(d) From the same note, repeated. This preceding note is called the note of preparation, and the appoggiatura becomes a "suspension," a term which will be discussed in a later chapter:

Ex. 82

3. *Chromatic passing notes.* These notes move by semitones, and must so proceed until a harmony note is reached. The notation may be chosen from the melodic chromatic scale, in which the notes are raised by sharps when ascending, and lowered by flats when descending, or better, the harmonic chromatic scale, which the student should understand.

The first example in the following is not very good, because the chromatic movement is not maintained until a harmony note is reached:

Ex. 83

Chromatic passing notes may be used in two parts at once, but the student should use them sparingly unless he is sure of the musical effect:

Ex. 84

4. *Changing notes.* If one auxiliary note is followed by another before returning to the note of the chord, changing notes occur. These are better confined to the soprano, and to dominant harmony, although they may be used over any chord. Sometimes the harmony notes are a third apart, when the auxiliary notes producing the changing notes are both lower, or both upper auxiliaries. The following patterns are those most commonly used. In the last example the first harmony note is omitted — this idiom is useful when triplet figures are a feature of the music:

Ex. 85

5. *Anticipations.* An anticipation is a note of a chord introduced before the chord itself. It should be used in the soprano only, and usually in the cadence. Sometimes, but rarely, anticipations of passing and auxiliary notes are used:

Ex. 85a

6. *Harmonization of melodies containing unessential notes:*
    The general harmonic basis should be that of not more than two chords to the bar. The unessential notes in the melody should first be marked, remembering that no matter how great a leap may be made to a note, if it moves on by step, it can be an unessential note. The changing note pattern is readily recognizable and is an apparent exception to the rule just given. The notes chosen as unessential notes should leave sufficient harmony notes to permit the use of good harmonic progressions. A few unessential notes may be introduced in the added parts, but not at the same time as those in the melody, except in the case of unaccented passing and auxiliary notes.

    Here is a melody with several unessential notes, harmonized as suggested above:

Ex. 86

7. *Figuring of unessential notes.* Figuring of unessential notes should cause no trouble, if the general rules are observed. Unessential notes are best in the soprano or alto, and figures indicate the distance above the bass note. A dash after a figure represents the continuation of one or more notes:

Ex. 87

EXERCISES

Aim for *neatness* and *accuracy.*

Harmonize the following melodies in three- or four-part harmony as desired, considering some notes as being unessential:

CHAPTER XIII

MODULATION

1. *Modulation* refers to the process of passing from one key to another, and this is one of the most vital factors in musical composition. Music without modulation would become very monotonous. Sixteen bars of music in the same key can only be tolerated if there is sufficient diversity of rhythmic interest to compensate for the lack of modulation. Very few folk songs, or hymn tunes, short as they are, remain in one key throughout, but pass through one or more keys closely associated with the original.

Modulation may be made from any key to any other key, but the most natural modulations are those which move to the so-called related keys.

2. *Related Keys.* It has already been established that major and minor keys are grouped in pairs having the same key-signature, and known as relative major or relative minor of each other. A larger group of keys may now be grouped, using as a basis the primary triads of any given major or minor key. If the three primary triads of a major key, with the relative minor of each of these are grouped together, it will be found that they consist of the first six triads of C major; also six triads of A minor (melodic scale) in descending form:

Ex. 88

(a) Since each of the above triads may be used as a tonic triad in its own right, there are five keys related to C + : D −, E − F +, G + , A − . Similarly to the key of A − these five keys are related: G + , F + , E − , D − , C +.

(b) Another formula may be used to find related keys:

	to C +	to A −
The dominant key and its relative (major or minor)	G + and E −	E − and G +

The subdominant key and its relative	F + and D −	D − and F +
The relative key (major or minor) of the given key.	A −	C +

(c) A third method of finding relative keys may help: Keys whose signatures differ by not more than one sharp or flat from the original are said to be related. For example, B ♭+ has two flats: The keys with one, two and three flats are F +, D −, G −, E ♭+, C −. B − has two sharps: The keys with one, two and three sharps are E −, G +, D ♯, A +, and F ♯−.

3. *Gradual Modulation.* Modulation to a related key may be made by one of the following formulae:

(a) Ia of the first key. A pivot chord. V7 and I of the new key.

(b) Ia of the first key. A pivot chord. Cadential six-four, V7 and Ia of new key.

The only chord which requires explanation is the pivot chord — a chord which should be common to both keys. This pivot chord may usually be found by choosing from the following chords the first that is common to both keys: II, IV, VI, or Ib of the new key. The first three chords may be used in root position or first inversion (except IIa in the minor key). Ib is suggested, because Ia is not good before the final cadence.

In modulation to the supertonic minor, it is most effective to use IVa or IVb of the new key instead of a pivot chord.

The dominant seventh may be used in root position or inversions in formula (a) above. Here are examples of gradual modulation, each of which should be studied carefully by the student:

Ex. 89

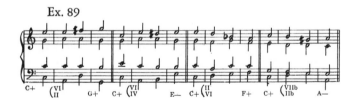

C+ (VI / II) G+ C+ (VII / IV) E− C+ (II / VI) F+ C+ (VIIb / IIb) A−

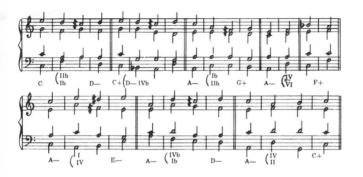

4. *Transition.* or sudden modulation. A transition is made by the omission of the pivot chord, so that the music moves at once to the new key without a connecting chord. This produces a chromatic change, that is, movement by chromatic semitone; and this chromatic move should be made in the same voice, otherwise false relation occurs. In writing transitions it is often desirable to invert the dominant seventh, so that the bass moves smoothly. Transitions are not good at cadences, but are excellent when used during the course of a phrase:

Ex. 90

5. *Continuous modulation in sentences.* In a sentence of eight bars a modulation may occur at the end of the first phrase. Modulations are good at cadences because they use the cadential progression V7 to I. A transition during the course of a phrase is particularly good, when made to a key which itself becomes a pivot key to that ultimately

reached by the modulation at the end of the phrase. For example, if a phrase modulates from Bb major to F major, the pivot chord (according to section 3) is G minor. Now if a transition is made to G minor, establishing the pivot chord as a key, the effect is excellent:

Ex. 91

In harmonizing melodies, the presence of an accidental usually indicates a modulation. If an eight bar melody starts and ends in C major, an F sharp may indicate a modulation to G major or to E minor; if G major is required, the F sharp must rise, because it is the leading note. It it falls to E, the key of E minor is suggested. Similarly B flat would suggest a modulation to the key of F major, and C sharp would suggest D minor

A sharpened note is usually, but not always, the leading note of a new key, and a flattened note is the subdominant of a new key.

Here is a melody with accidentals. The harmony is not written in, but the keys through which it passes are indicated. The bracketed portions should be harmonized by V7 — I or V7 — VI in the keys named:

Ex. 92

Sometimes a modulation is made during the course of a phrase and confirmed at the end. Here is a passage modulating from D + to A + , but the new dominant seventh in bar 2 moves to VIa instead of Ia, which is reserved for the cadence:

Ex. 93

Notice that it is not imperative to have the seventh of V7 present on the accented beat. It may very well be delayed to move as a passing note, or it may be omitted altogether, if preceded by a cadential six-four.

Melodies without accidentals sometimes imply modulations, in which the accidentals will appear in some of the lower parts. Unless the student can hear the harmony mentally he may not always sense the implied modulation. Bearing in mind, however, that at least one modulation should be used in a sentence, and sometimes two or three, it is a good plan to try to reach the dominant key at the middle cadence.

Sentences of sixteen bars are known as binary sentences, because they contain two periods of eight bars, or four phrases. The following plan is suggested for modulations: Phrase 1: No modulation. Phrase 2: Through one key to reach the dominant key. Phrase 3: Through the subdominant and its relative minor (in either order): Phrase 4: In the tonic key without modulation.

In a sentence in C major: Bars 1 — 4 in C + ; 5 — 8 through A – to G + ; 9 — 12 through D – to F + ; 13 — 16 in C +.

Here is a melody of sixteen bars with no accidentals, but the plan suggested above is followed, and the modulating chords are written in:—

Ex. 94

6. *How to figure basses involving modulation.* If the modulations suggested by an unfigured bass are figured first, the remainder of the bass will cause the student no trouble.

Here are some suggestions that usually work:

(a) If the bass moves up a fourth or down a fifth, use V̇7a — Ia of the key suggested:

Ex. 95

(b) If the bass moves up a semitone, use V7b to Ia; or V7c — Ib in a minor key:

Ex. 96

(c) If the bass moves up a tone, use V7c to Ib in a major key:

Ex. 97

(d) If the bass falls a diatonic semitone use V7d in a major key:

Ex. 98

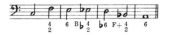

(e) If the bass falls a tone, use V7d in a minor key:

Ex. 99

After the above possible progressions have been determined and the proper figuring used, the remainder of the bass is usually capable

of holding simple chords — a mixture of triads and **first inversion**.
A long dominant note at the end of any phrase suggests a cadential
six-four followed by Va or V7a, or V7d.

The following bass with figures to indicate the modulations should
illustrate the above technique:

Ex. 100

EXERCISES

Aim for *neatness* and *accuracy*. Be careful to insert the proper
accidentals.

1. Modulate gradually, using not more than five chords, between
the following keys:

A + to B−   E♭+ to C −   G + to E−   D♭+ to G♭+
D + to A+   G− to B♭+   F − to C−   B♭− to D♭+
F + to D−   A♭+ to E♭+   E − to D+   A♭+ to D♭+
F♯− to E+   D − to A −   C♯− to B+   F♯+ to C♯+
E + to B+   C − to A♭+   B − to F♯−   A − to G +

2. Modulate suddenly between these keys:

A − to D−   E + to C♯−   F + to G −   F − to B♭−
B − to E−   F♯+ to D♯−   F♯+ to G♯−   C − to F −

3. Harmonize the following figured basses in four parts:

4. Harmonize the following melodies in four parts:

-MEMO-

CHAPTER XIV

SECONDARY SEVENTHS

1. When a seventh is added to a triad other than the dominant triad, the chord becomes a secondary, or diatonic seventh. The dominant seventh is sometimes called a primary seventh. All chords of the seventh are named from the root on which they are constructed, such as tonic seventh, supertonic seventh, etc. Here are the secondary sevenths in C major:

Ex. 101

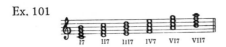

In minor keys, these are the only effective secondary sevenths:

Ex. 102

Unlike the dominant seventh, which is the same in major and minor keys, secondary sevenths are different. It will be noticed from a careful examination of each of the above chords that in some, the third and seventh are major, while in others the third and seventh are minor, and there are also some with a diminished fifth. It is not necessary to memorize the particular construction of each chord, as they are all treated in a similar manner.

2. *Resolution of secondary sevenths.* When any one of the secondary sevenths is played on the piano it sounds somewhat harsh, and much more discordant than the dominant seventh. This harshness is modified to some extent by writing a chord before the secondary seventh which uses the discordant note of the latter as a concord. This is known as *preparation* of the seventh, although it is really preparation of the ear to accept the seventh. The preparation of the seventh

should take place in the same voice. The seventh must also resolve by falling one step, usually to a note which becomes the third of the new chord:

Ex. 103

3. *The supertonic seventh.* This is by far the most important of all the secondary sevenths, because it resolves naturally to the dominant chord and thus makes an excellent approach to the imperfect, deceptive and perfect cadences. The seventh of II7 falls to the note which becomes the third of the dominant seventh.

Since the dominant seventh may be preceded' by a cadential six-four, the resolution of the II7 may pass through a cadential six-four before resolving; furthermore, the II7 may resolve to the ordinary Va without the seventh:

Ex. 104

4. *Sequences of secondary sevenths.* Other secondary sevenths are useful in sequential patterns in the major key. It has already been stated that the seventh falls one step to a note that becomes the third of the new chord — but this chord need not be a triad; it may be another chord of the seventh. In such a process of resolution, a chain of sevenths is produced in sequence:

Ex. 105

5. *Inversions of secondary sevenths.* These chords, like dominant sevenths have three inversions, and the figuring is the same as that used for the dominant seventh. No confusion of chords arises if the root of the chord is discovered.

Second inversions are rare. The other two inversions are frequently used. The first inversion of II7 makes a better approach to a cadence than the root position, as it allows the bass to move smoothly. It is equally good in minor keys:

Ex. 106

Inversions of secondary sevenths are good in a sequential chain of sevenths, when the first and third inversions alternate:

Ex. 107

6. *Special resolutions of some secondary sevenths.* In addition to the standard form of resolution in which the seventh falls to become the third of the next chord, there are some resolutions used in order to avoid weak chords.

In these special cases, the seventh of the diatonic sevenths need not be prepared.

(a) IV7 may resolve on Va or Vb, or on a cadential six-four:

Ex. 108

(b) VI7 may resolve to V7, but care must be taken that the soprano and bass do not move in consecutive sevenths. The following idiom should be memorized. Notice that the melodic minor scale is used to avoid an augmented second in the bass:

Ex. 109

VI7a V7b   VI7a V7b

(c) VII7 is frequently called the leading seventh, because it is built on the leading note. In the minor key it is called the diminished seventh. These chords will be more fully discussed in the next chapter, but it may be said at present that they may resolve directly to the tonic, or first pass through the dominant seventh.

Ex. 110

VII7a Ia   VII7a V7b   VII7a Ia

7. *The chord of the added sixth.* If the first inversion of the supertonic seventh is considered from another angle a chord of the added sixth is produced. For example, if in the following chord:

Ex. 111

F is considered as the root, instead of D, it becomes IVa with a sixth added above instead of a supertonic seventh. This may be more clearly understood if a study of a following progression is made:

Ex. 112

6
5

64

The first chord of the above is IVa and the last is Ia, forming a plagal cadence. In the second chord nothing is changed except the treble, which may be considered as a passing note. The combination on the second chord is then IVa with the sixth added. The figuring is $\begin{smallmatrix}6\\5\end{smallmatrix}$

The added sixth on IV should be treated as follows:

(a) Precede it by IVa if possible.

(b) The sixth from the bass should be in the soprano and should rise one step.

(c) It moves to Ia and makes an ornamental form of the plagal cadence.

Ex.113

Occasionally the added sixth is written above I, and this resolves to Va, making an ornamental form of an imperfect cadence:

Ex. 114

The following additional points are worth remembering:—The fifth of any secondary seventh may be omitted, and the root doubled, when the chord is in its root position. Inversions of all chords should be complete.

Secondary sevenths may be used as pivot chords in modulation. For example, II7 in G major is the same as VI7 of C major, therefore a modulation from C to G may be made as follows:

Ex. 115

EXERCISES

Aim for *neatness* and *accuracy*.

1. Prepare and resolve the following chords:
   II7a in G+ , B− , E− , A♭+ , D− , F♯+ .
   II7b in B♭+ , A+ , E+ , C♯− , D♭+ , G−

2. Write the added sixth on the subdominant in these keys: with

a preceding and succeeding chord in each case.

E♭+ , A+ , G♯− , B♭− , D+ , F+ , E−.

3. Harmonize the following figured basses in four parts:

4. Harmonize the following melodies in four parts, using secondary sevenths where appropriate:

5. Add three parts above each of these unfigured basses:

CHAPTER XV

DOMINANT DISCORDS

1. It is well known that the progression Va to Ia is one of the strongest of all musical combinations, and makes a definite full close to any sentence. By adding the seventh to Va the progression is further intensified as the presence of the dominant seventh demands resolution, which is naturally found in Ia.

It now becomes possible to add other notes above a dominant seventh until all the notes of the major or minor scales have been used in a series of superimposed thirds:

Ex. 116

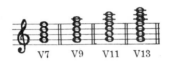

2. *The dominant ninth.* In the previous example it will be seen that there are five notes in this chord. In four part harmony the fifth of the chord is omitted. Unlike the dominant seventh, the dominant ninth is not identical in the major and minor keys:— the ninth is major in a major key, and minor in a minor key.

The ninth must resolve, since it is a discord. This resolution is similar to that of the dominant seventh, so that the seventh and ninth fall and the third rises. The natural resolution is to Ia with the root of V9 moving up or down to the tonic. The V9– is good in the major key as well as the minor, but the reverse is not true: The V9 + cannot be used in the minor key:

Of the above chords, the dominant seventh has already been fully discussed. The dominant eleventh has no practical value. It therefore remains to consider the dominant ninth and thirteenth respectively:

Ex. 117

The dominant ninth may also resolve to the secondary seventh on VI (VI7) which in turn resolves to V7b, and then to the tonic:

Ex. 118

The dominant major ninth is only good if it is above the third; this forces it to be used in the soprano or alto only.

There are no available inversions of the dominant ninth, as the root heard against the ninth sounds very harsh when it is not in the bass.

Dominant ninths are very rarely used and do not make good final cadences.

3. *Derivatives of the dominant ninth.* If the root of the dominant ninth is eliminated, a new chord is formed — the leading seventh in the major key and the diminished seventh in the minor key. These chords were mentioned in the preceding chapter when discussing secondary sevenths. They now become more important chords as dominant discords. Here are the dominant major and minor ninths with their derivatives, showing their symbols:

Ex. 119

V9+   VII7   V9—   VII7o

4. *The leading seventh.* This chord is good in major keys only, since .the dominant major ninth is only good in major keys. It seldom forms a satisfactory cadence, but is quite good when used anywhere else. It resolves naturally on tonic harmony.

The seventh and fifth both fall and the leading note rises. Care must be taken to keep the seventh (the original ninth) above the leading note, unless the seventh is prepared, otherwise it is harsh. The Fifth *may* rise if the chord is in first inversion and resolves to Ib.

In resolving discords there are several prohibited consecutive intervals. The following should be avoided, as they are all modifications of consecutive octaves:

7 — 8, 8 — 7, 8 — 9, 9 — 8:

Ex. 120

Here are the natural resolutions of the VII7. Notice that the seventh is prepared in the third inversion of this chord, because it is below the leading note; also it must pass through a V7 to avoid resolution to a six-four, which must not be preceded by a chord containing the leading note:

Ex. 121

5. *The diminished seventh.* This chord is formed by the omission of the root from the dominant minor ninth, and consists of three minor thirds above the leading note. It is good in any key — major or minor. The resolutions are the same as those of the leading seventh. The third of the chord is free to move to any note of the next chord. As in VII7, it is necessary to resolve the third inversion of this chord to the dominant seventh before proceeding to the tonic. Here are the resolutions of the diminished seventh and its inversions in C minor — these chords are equally good when resolved in C major:

Ex. 122

The diminished seventh may be used as a substitute for the dominant seventh in modulations and transitions. On account of its peculiar construction, with all its notes equidistant, it can be used enharmonically, by changing the name of one of the notes of the chord, so that it can at once be adapted for use in another key. The following will be readily understood if each sentence is studied carefully:

(a) The diminished seventh is built on the leading note of the minor key and has three inversions.

(b) Since all its notes are equidistant, any one of these notes may become a leading note of another key.

(c) Since each of the four notes may be considered as a leading note, the diminished seventh may be used in four keys.

(d) Since the notes of the diminished seventh are a minor third from each other, the four keys are also a minor third, or multiples thereof, from each other.

From the above it is apparent that the diminished seventh of C minor is available also a A minor, F sharp minor and D sharp minor (or E flat minor). To prove that these chords with changed notation can be so used, here is an illustration:

Ex. 123

Since a diminished seventh chord may be written in four different keys by the enharmonic change of one or more notes, it is obvious that it may be used as a pivot chord — approached as belonging to one key and left as belonging to one of the three others, major or minor, and thus is very useful in transition:

Ex. 124

6. *The dominant thirteenth.* By referring to the chart in paragraph (1) it will be seen that the V13 contains seven notes. In four part harmony the notes that best define the chord are the root, third, seventh and thirteenth.

These chords are generally reserved for cadences. Here are the rules for resolution:

(a) The thirteenth must be in the soprano.

(b) The thirteenth resolves by falling a third.

(c) The seventh falls one step, and the third rises a semitone.

(d) V13 in root position must resolve to Ia or VIa.

(e) There are only two satisfactory inversions:

The first inversion has the third in the bass, and the third inversion has the seventh in the bass.

(f) The inversions follow the above rules in resolution, excepting that they cannot resolve on VIa, only on Ia, or in the case of the third inversion, on Ib.

Here is the V13 and its two inversions in C major:

Ex. 125

V13a   Ia   V13a   VIa   V13b   Ia   V13c   Ib

When the dominant thirteenth is in the minor key, the thirteenth is minor, but its treatment is the same as in major keys:

Ex. 126

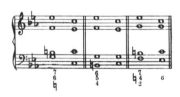

The dominant minor thirteenth may be used in the major key, but the thirteenth is usually changed enharmonically to become an augmented twelfth. This note rises a semitone in resolution, causing the major third of Ia to be doubled, a somewhat unusual feature:

71

Ex. 127

EXERCISES

Aim for *neatness* and *accuracy*.

1. Write and resolve the following chords in the keys specified:
V9 in F +, G−, D+, B−, F#−, Bb +.
VII7 and its inversions in G +, B+, A b+, D b+.
VII7o and its inversions in A−, D−, G−, C #−.
V13 and inversions in A +, G+, D−, B−.

2. Write transitions, using VII7o between these keys:
C + to A ÷, Eb+ to C −, E ⊤ to C #−, B+ to C ♮−, D b+ to
E b− ;

3. Add three parts above the following basses:

4. Harmonize the following melodies:

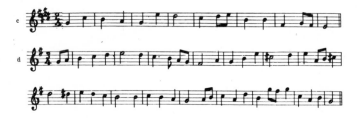

- M·E M O -

CHAPTER XVI

SUSPENSIONS

1. A suspension is a device sometimes employed during a chord change, in which one voice retains its original note, while the other voices proceed to their respective parts of the second chord. This causes a discord, which is resolved by means of the suspended note proceeding to the delayed chord note, falling or rising one step.

Ex. 128

The chords used above are V7a — Ia. In example (a) the note D in the soprano makes a suspension over the tonic chord in the second bar. It is prepared in the same voice by being part of the preceding chord. It falls one step in resolution. At (b) the suspension is in the alto: F is prepared by occurring in the preceding chord, and resolves by falling one step. Note the absence of a tie — it is not imperative that a suspended note be tied. At (c) the previous suspensions are now combined. Notice that in (a) and (c) the leading note moves down to the dominant, because the note which resolves a discord should not be doubled against the suspension except in the bass. At (d) there is another double suspension with one note rising in resolution; this is quite normal because the suspended note is the leading note. The last example (e) combines the three suspensions.

2. *Single suspensions.* Since a common chord contains three different notes, it is possible for each of these notes to be displaced by an upper or lower auxiliary note, and therefore six different suspensions are possible, though not all equally effective. Here are the six suspended notes written over the chord of C (implied):

Of the above, the most important are the 9 8 and the 4 3 suspensions. The 6 5 usually occurs in the treble, and the 2 3 and the 7 8 are generally used in combination with one another. The 4 5 is not musical. Note that the figuring of suspensions must be indicated horizontally.

3. *Rules for the treatment of suspensions.* The following rules must be memorized and retained so that music which is ornamented by suspensions will not sound harsh. Suspensions, when properly used, and combined with unessential notes, are of great value in producing a good musical texture.

(a) A progression must be correct in itself before suspensions can be introduced.

(b) The note of preparation should be of equal or greater value than the note of suspension, if the notes are tied together. If not tied, the first note may be shorter.

(c) The note on which the suspension resolves should not be doubled in any other part except as the bass of a 9 8. An exception to this is allowed when the note of resolution is I, IV or V, and is approached and left by step in contrary motion: (Doubling must never occur in a part above the suspension).

Ex. 130

4. *The 9 8 suspension and its inversions.* The figuring for this suspension in root position is 9 8 or sometimes **9 8** The short
5 —
3 —

lines, it will be remembered, indicate the continuation of the 5 and 3 while 9 moves to 8. This suspension may occur in any one of the voices above the bass, but it should never be so close to the bass as to form a 2 1, which is harsh.

Ex. 131.

If a triad is written in first inversion with the suspension of the root still attached, the result is a 7 6. This is best used in the soprano because the 6 from the bass is usually the most satisfactory soprano note. Here are some examples:

Ex. 1'32

The second inversion of a 9 8 suspension is generally associated with a cadential six-four and is figured $\frac{6}{5}\frac{-}{4}$. The suspension is best used in the soprano part and since the chord is a six-four, the bass must be doubled:

Ex. 133

It may seem strange to say that a triad has three inversions, but when the root is doubled, with a 9 8 attached to one note of these, there are four possible bass notes, the root, third, fifth and the suspended root. The suspension, when used in the bass is figured $\frac{4}{2}\frac{-}{}$. These figures must not be confused with $\frac{4}{2}$ without the dashes, used for any chord of the seventh in its third inversion. In the following examples, it will be seen that the dashes indicate, as usual, that the upper parts are to be held while the bass moves. Care must be taken not to double the root, which is now suspended in the bass:

Ex. 134

5. *The* 4 3 *suspension.* The figuring is 4 3 or sometimes $\begin{smallmatrix}5 &-\\4 & 3\end{smallmatrix}$
Sometimes it is necessary to omit the fifth and triple the bass when
the suspension is used on Ia. This suspension is good in any part.
Here are some examples of the 4 3 used in each upper part:

The first inversion of the 4 3 suspension places the suspension
in the bass, because it is attached to the third of the chord. This
is often preceded by the third inversion of the dominant seventh,
and is figured $\begin{smallmatrix}5 &-\\2 & -\end{smallmatrix}$. Since neither the suspension nor its resolution
may be doubled, it becomes necessary to double the 2 or 5 above the
bass, as these notes become 3 and 6 when the suspension resolves:

Ex. 136

The second inversion of the 4 3 is associated with a six-four chord,
usually cadential. The bass must be doubled and the suspension is
best in the soprano. The figuring is $\begin{smallmatrix}7 & 6\\4 & -\end{smallmatrix}$:

Ex. 137

6. *Other single suspensions.*

(a) The 6 5 suspension is better used in the soprano and on tonic or dominant harmony. Like many other suspensions, the second inversion is used in connection with a six-four chord. Here is the 6 5 with its first and second inversions and their proper figuring:

Ex. 137a

(b) The 7 8 and the 2 3 suspensions are rarely used singly, but here is an example of each. They are best used in the soprano, and can never be used in the bass. Rising suspensions in the bass are extremely harsh:

Ex. 138

7. *Double suspensions.* Many suspensions may be combined, and are very effective, provided the interval of a fourth is not used consecutively between any two parts above the bass. When the bass is stationary, the tenor becomes the lowest moving part, and must be treated as a temporary bass. The following is not good, with consecutive fourths between the soprano and the tenor:

Ex. 139

78

The best combination of two suspensions are as follows:

```
9 8      7 6      7 8      9 8      7 6      7 8
4 3,     5 4,     4 3,     7 8,     5 6,     2 3.
```

The above suspensions are sufficient for ordinary use, and the student who is able to use any of these will have an excellent command of harmony. Here is an example of each used in the progression V7 — Ia:

Ex. 140

8. *Triple suspensions.* The following are the only triple- suspensions which are practical, the first of which is frequently used at the final cadence:

```
9 8      7 8      9 8
7 8      6 5      7 6
4 3,     4 3,     4 3.
```

Ex. 141

9. *Ornamental resolutions.* Any suspension may be resolved ornamentally by interpolating a note or notes between the discord and its resolution. This ornamentation may be formed by (a) using another note of the same chord, or (b) a pair of eighth notes moving upwards or downwards by step:

Ex. 142

10. An *appoggiatura* is an unprepared suspension, or conversely, a suspension is a prepared appoggiatura. These have already been discussed in Chapter XII and need no more than a passing reference. Any of the aforementioned suspensions may be used without preparation and thus they become appoggiaturas:

Ex. 143

11. *The use of suspensions in harmonizing melodies or basses.* A suspension may be introduced whenever a note falls a second, and occasionally when a note rises a second, unless that note be in the bass.

Suspensions used in moderation, with ornamental resolutions and occasional passing notes give a richer texture to the music, and prevent that angularity that is associated with certain types of Victorian hymn tunes. If the student compares such hymn tunes with the chorales of Bach, he will see at once what gives the majestic character to the latter.

Here is a short phrase written with correct harmony in plain chords:

Ex. 144

The same harmonic basis may be decorated with suspensions and passing notes to become an elaborate passage such as this:

Ex. 145

EXERCISES

Aim for *neatness* and *accuracy*.

1. Ornament the following by using suspensions and passing notes where effective:

2. Harmonize the following melodies, using suspensions where convenient:

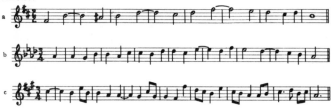

3. Add three parts above the following figured basses:

CHAPTER XVII

CHROMATIC SEVENTHS AND NINTHS

1. *Chromatic chords in general.*

All chords thus far discussed have been built of notes of the diatonic scales, major or minor. If the harmonic chromatic scale is used for chord construction, several chromatic chords become available. Chromatic chords require one or more accidentals in their formation.

The harmonic chromatic scale has been discussed in the author's Basis of Music. Its construction is easily remembered, since the tonic and dominant of the scale occur once only, and all other notes twice. Whereas it is used as a basis of chromatic harmony, it is conversely true that if a series of primary minor ninth chords are written, the accidentals used in their construction produce the correct notation for the harmonic chromatic scale. A primary ninth is one built on I, II, and V with a major third, perfect fifth, minor seventh and minor ninth. Here are the three primary ninths of C + :

Ex. 146

These chords resolve naturally on the chords of IVa, Va and Ia, the three primary triads of the key. The accidentals used in the above primary ninths are now used in forming the semitones of the harmonic chromatic scale with the scale of C major as the basis:

Ex. 147

2. *Chromatic supertonic seventh.* (ChII7)

This chord is constructed on the supertonic with the intervals conforming to those of

82

a dominant seventh: major 3, perfect 5, and minor 7 so that the ChII7 of C is exactly the same as the V7 of G, but its resolution is different:

Ex. 148

If the chord resolves to the tonic of G major a modulation takes place, which is quite the proper thing if such is desired. However if the chord is considered a chromatic chord in C, it must resolve in the key of C without modulation. This is done in one of two ways:

(a) Resolution to the V7 of C, or (b) to a cadential six-four in C. The 7th should fall if possible or remain stationary, and the other notes move as smoothly as possible. If the chord is in root position the fifth may be omitted and the root doubled.

Ex. 149

Chromatic chords used in the major key are also good in the tonic minor key. The intervals must be the same in both keys, but the notation varies because of the difference in the key-signature. Here is ChII7 in C minor:

Ex. 150

If required for modulation, the ChII7 may be approached as such in one key and left as the V7 in another key, or vice versa. thus becoming a pivot chord:

Ex. 151

C+: ChII7   C+: V7
G+: V7   Ia   F+: ChII7   V7   Ia

Since ChII7 has II for its root it makes an excellent approach to the imperfect, deceptive or perfect cadences. It may, like all other chords, be decorated by a suspension or an appoggiatura:

Ex. 151a

Ch II7   Ch II7

3. *The chromatic supertonic ninth.* (ChII9) This chord is formed by adding a major ninth above the ChII7 in a major key, or a minor ninth in minor keys, although the latter form is also good in the major key.

The fifth is omitted. The major ninth should be above the third. There are no inversions. The chord resolves to a dominant seventh or to a cadential six-four. It may also be used as a pivot chord in modulation, since its construction is the same as that of the V9:

Ex. 152

Ch II9+   Ch II9

4. *Derivatives of the chromatic supertonic ninths.* If the root is omitted, the following chords are produced:

Ex. 153

xIV7 is very rarely used, but the *diminished seventh on the raised subdominant* (xIV7o) is of very common occurrence, and is perhaps the most useful of all chromatic chords. xIV7 resolves in the same way as xIV7o, but the latter is here discussed more fully. It has three special uses:

(a) As a precadential chord, resolving on the V7 or a cadential six-four. The notes should move as smoothly as possible, and the seventh should fall a semitone, rise a chromatic semitone, or remain stationary:

Ex. 154

(b) As a modulating chord, when it is approached from any chord in the original key. In such cases xIV7o should belong to the new key and resolve as shown in the previous examples. Here are some extreme modulations, showing the smooth movement, and the possibility of any chord of approach:

Ex. 155

(c) As a decorative chord placed between two statements of Ia or Ib in major keys only.

The following rules must be observed:

1. Double the fifth of the tonic chord.

2. Change the seventh of xIV7o enharmonically, so that the result appears as three auxiliary notes with the other note remaining stationary:

Ex. 156

5. *The chromatic tonic seventh.* (ChI7). This chord is constructed with the same intervals as the dominant seventh and the chromatic supertonic seventh, but on the tonic root, so that it appears as the dominant seventh of the subdominant key:

Ex. 157

It has two special uses: (a) an approach to dominant or supertonic chromatic harmony:

Ex. 158

(b) As a modulating chord, when it may be approached as a tonic seventh and left as a supertonic or dominant seventh of the new key as follows:

Ex. 159

86

6. *The chromatic tonic ninth.* (ChI9). This chord is very rarely used. It is never inverted, and does not make a good cadence with anything. If used at all, it should be followed by ChII7 or V7 harmony:

Ex. 160

7. *The diminished seventh from the tonic minor ninth*:

Ex. 161

This chord is rarely used except as a decorative chord between two statements of Va or Vb, and as such it gives colour to the harmony. In writing this progression, it is necessary to double the fifth in Va or Vb, and change both the fifth and the seventh of the diminished seventh chord enharmonically, so that the result is three auxiliary notes, with one note remaining stationary:

Ex. 161a

8. *The supertonic seventh with lowered fifth.* (IIo7). This chord is really a diatonic seventh of the minor key, borrowed for use in the major, when it becomes chromatic by the use of the diminished fifth. Since it has a supertonic root it resolves naturally to the dominant seventh or a cadential six-four:

Ex. 162

9. The chromatic sevenths should be used sparingly. They are colourful chords, but care must be taken not to force them into places where they do not fit naturally.

ChII7 and IIo7 are best reserved for use before a cadence, and they should then move to a cadential six-four if possible.

xIV7o is also good before a cadence, but if used as a decorative chord, it may occur at the beginning of any phrase. The same is true of III7o, which may be used near the beginning if Va or Vb are chosen as opening chords.

It should be said also, that while rules governing the resolution of the seventh in chromatic chords are not quite so strict as in dominant sevenths, the beginner is advised to make the discordant notes fall if possible. If this cannot be done, they may rise a semitone or remain stationary. The seventh should not rise more than a semitone except in one special case, when the seventh of ChII7 may rise a third in this idiom, resolving on a cadential six-four:

Ex. 163

EXERCISES

Aim for *neatness* and *accuracy*.

1. Write and resolve the ChII7 in two ways in each of these keys:
A +, B −, C #− , D ♭+ .

2. Write and resolve the ChII9 in E +, G −, B ♭− , F + .

3. Write and resolve ChI7 in A ♭+ , D +, B − .

4. Write and resolve the xIV7o in two different ways in F −, F #− , B +, G ♭+ .

5. Write and resolve III7o as a decoration of dominant harmony in G +, E +, A ♭+ and D ♭+ .

6. Modulate from G + to D +; A ♭+ to E ♭+ ; A − to E −; C #− to G #− . In each case use ChII7 of the first key as the pivot chord.

7. Modulate from F + to B ♭+ ; D + to G +; E − to A −. In each case use ChII7 of the first key as the pivot chord.

8. Modulate to the keys given in question 7, using ChII7 of the second key as the pivot chord

9. Add three parts to the following basses:

10. Harmonize the following melodies:

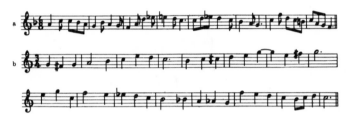

- MEMO -

CHAPTER XVIII

CHROMATIC SIXTHS

1. *Augmented sixth chords.* These chords are built on the minor II or the minor VI of the scale, usually the latter. Since students may wonder why chromatic notes are chosen for roots of these chords the following may help:

Ex. 164

In the progression at (a) the D flat in the bass is a chromatic passing note between V7c and Ia. The combination above the D flat, is known as an augmented sixth chord, because of the interval of an augmented sixth from D flat to B; at (b) the A flat in the bass is a chromatic passing note between a ChII7c and V7 (with an appoggiatura in the soprano), and another chord of the augmented sixth is formed. These are the two augmented sixth chords of C major or C minor built on -II or -VI as stated above.

There are three forms of augmented sixths, known as the Italian, French and German sixth respectively (It6, Fr6, Gn6.):

Ex. 165

The above are all built on the minor VI of the scale, and there is an augmented sixth above each, which need not necessarily be in the soprano as shown. Each chord has the tonic of C major as a note to hold it to the key. They differ by one note only:

(a) The third is doubled in the Italian sixth.
(b) The supertonic is added in the French sixth.
(c) The minor mediant is added in the German sixth.

In the resolution, the augmented sixth expands to an octave — the bass falls a semitone and the augmented sixth rises a semitone. The other notes move as smoothly as possible. The Italian and French sixths resolve to Va or V7a, but the German sixth, while it may move to V7, usually resolves to a cadential six-four. If it moves to a dominant seventh, consecutive fifths occur, but these are always allowed as they do not sound objectionable. Here are the three chords already discussed with the resolutions and the proper figuring:

Ex. 166

The figuring of the Fr6 and Gn6 should not be confused with that of chords of the seventh since the accidentals change the character of the chords.

2. *Augmented sixths in minor keys.* These chords are the same in a major key and its tonic minor, but the figuring is different, because of the key signature. Here is the series built on the minor sixth of C minor. Compare the figuring with that of the same chords in C major in the last paragraph. Notice the sixth degree of a minor key is already minor and therefore needs no accidental:

Ex. 167

3. *Augmented sixths on the minor second of the scale.* The three forms of the augmented sixth may occur on -II but the musical result is not so good, except when used near the end of a composition,

where they are quite satisfactory. They resolve naturally on tonic harmony, and the consecutive fifths produced by the German sixth proceeding to its resolution are tolerated:

Ex. 168

4. *Inversions of augmented sixths.* The Italian sixth is never inverted. The French sixth is sometimes used in first inversion; but the German sixth becomes most impressive when used in its third inversion, and makes a really good approach to a cadential six-four in a cadence. Here are some inversions with their resolutions. The last example is the best. Notice the figuring, which must not be mistaken for that of a chord of the seventh:

Ex. 169

5 .*Enharmonic change of the German 6th.* If the German sixth on -VI in C is played on the piano it sounds like a dominant seventh in D flat, unless it is resolved as an augmented sixth. When the sixth of the chord is changed enharmonically it becomes a minor seventh, and as such is part of a dominant seventh chord. Here is the German sixth of C with the augmented sixth changed enharmonically to a minor seventh:

Ex. 170

Gn 6 in C=   V7 in D♭

From the above it is obvious that modulation may be made between keys a semitone apart by approaching the pivot chord as a German sixth in one key and leaving it as a dominant seventh in the other, or vice versa:

Ex. 171

6. *The Neapolitan sixth.* This chord is really a first inversion of a major triad on the minor II of the scale, for example the chord of D flat major used in C major or C minor. It is usually easier to comprehend if it is considered to be a chord built on IV with a minor third and minor sixth above it — F, A flat and D flat.

The sixth from the bass is the best soprano note. The third is not good in the soprano. The bass is the best note to double. In resolution, the third and sixth both fall — if it moves to a dominant seventh, the sixth falls a diminished third. The other resolution is to a cadential six-four, and then to dominant harmony.

The Neapolitan sixth (N6) may pass through the third inversion of a German sixth or through xIV7o before reaching the six-four.

When used in a minor key, if the N6 resolves into a cadential six-four and thence to dominant and tonic harmony, the result is known as a Pathetic cadence.

Ex. 172

7. *Chromatic triads.* In addition to the Neapolitan sixth, several other chromatic triads are also available. A triad becomes chromatic if it has one or two chromatic notes, but at least one note of the triad must belong to the key. For example, the triad of F sharp major is not available in C major because not one of the notes is found in C major. The triads best adapted for use in a given key are thus used in C major here:

Ex. 173

The simplest use is to insert them between two statements of another chord whose root is a minor second up or down:

Ex. 174

Chromatic triads may also be used wherever a diatonic triad is used — for example, instead of IIa to Va, it is quite good to use ChIIa, or -IIa, and instead of VIa, the major chord on -VI is good. The minor triad on IV is also a good precadential chord:

Ex. 175

This concludes the chromatic technique available for ordinary harmonic writing. It must again be emphasized that the best place for chromatic chords is just before the cadence, and they should only be used when strongly suggested by a chromatic note in the treble or bass.

EXERCISES

Aim for *neatness* and *accuracy*.

1. Write and resolve the Italian 6th on -VI in D+, A+, E−, B−, C ♯−, F ♯+

2. Write and resolve the French 6th on -VI in B ♭+ , G −, A −, D ♯− , E ♭+ , A ♭+

3. Write and resolve the German 6th on -VI in E + G ♯− , F −, B ♭− , F ♯+ E ♭−

4. Write and resolve the Italian, French and German 6ths on -II in E + and F −

5. Write and resolve the Neapolitan 6th in two ways in B + , E − , D ♭+ , D −

6. By enharmonic change of the German 6th into V7 modulate from E + to F + ; B − to C + ; F♯− to G − , A − to B ♭+.

7. Precede and follow each of the following chords by suitable chords in A + :

8. Add three parts above the following figured basses:

9. Harmonize the following melodies:

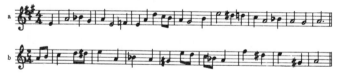

CHAPTER XIX

EXTRANEOUS MODULATION

1. *Conditions for modulation.* Modulation to any key other than the related keys already discussed, is said to be "extraneous" modulation. The same general plan is available as before:— there must be a pivot chord, preceded by a chord in the original key, and followed by some form of cadential harmony in the new key.

A key is said to be established when its dominant chord is followed by its tonic chord. It is not necessary that either chord should be in root position. In most cases the seventh is added to the dominant chord, and the cadential six-four may precede the dominant seventh, if desired. A six-four chord on the first beat of a bar is so strongly suggestive of a modulation that it should be followed by a cadence in the key of which the bass note of the six-four is the dominant.

In modulating from one key to another, the essential chord to keep in mind is the V7 of the new key; for example, in modulating from G minor to A major, E should be considered in the bass, with a V7 or cadential six-four moving to Va or V7 above it.

Modulation is classified as Diatonic, Chromatic or Enharmonic. Diatonic modulation occurs when the pivot chord is diatonic in both keys, or in either of them. In Chromatic modulation the pivot chord is chromatic in both keys. Enharmonic modulation occurs when at least one note is common to both keys, but under different names:

2. *Diatonic modulation.* There are three kinds of diatonic modulation:

(a) When the pivot chord is diatonic in both keys, This has been fully discussed in Chapter XIII. The pivot chord is II, IV, VI, or Ib of the new key. It is always best to keep the new key in mind when making any kind of modulation.

(b) When the pivot chord is diatonic in the original key but not in the new key. This type of modulation requires more thought. The student should use the pivot chord which moves smoothly and makes the best approach to the cadence in the new key:

Ex. 176

E♭+   V♭
A—   N6

(c) When the pivot chord is diatonic in the new key but not in the original key:

Ex. 177

E+   VI7
B—   II7

3. *Chromatic modulation.* This type of modulation requires a pivot chord which is chromatic in both keys, requiring an accidental in either key. Note that the accidental used for the leading note in minor keys is always regarded as being diatonic. There are many available chords for this form of modulation, but the best are those which make the strongest approach to the dominant seventh of the new key. There are three excellent chords for use, but if chromatic modulation is desired in the most effective way, the student must choose the one that is chromatic in both keys from:—

(a) The diminished seventh on the raised subdominant (xIV7o) of the new key. This chord is always correct, as it may be approached from any chord, therefore from any key. Its notation should be that of the new key, although it will always be found in the original key, with different notation. For example, in the following modulation from F to A♭, the xIV7o of A♭ is also in F as xIV7o, but the notation in F is B, D, F, and A♭, whereas in A♭ the chord is D, F, A♭ and C♭ (remembering that the notation of any diminished seventh is found by counting three minor thirds above the root):

Ex. 178

F+   ×IV7o   A♭+

97

The above modulation may appear to be enharmonic, but the function of the diminished seventh chord is chromatic in both keys and it remains the same type of chord in both keys, and is thus considered as chromatic rather than enharmonic.

(b) The German sixth on -VI. This chord should belong to the new key. It may be an extreme chord in the original key, but it is available for use if it has at least one note in that key:

Ex. 179

(c) The Neapolitan sixth in the new key. This chord is only good in chromatic modulation if it is also chromatic in the first key. Since it is the first inversions of a major triad it must be one of the accepted chromatic triads in the first key. It is more satisfactory when modulating to a minor key:

Ex. 180

4. *Enharmonic modulation.* This form of modulation implies that one note of the pivot chord or possibly of the dominant seventh of the new key must change its name either actually or mentally. In such cases the German sixth of the new key is often used.

It has already been stated that the German sixth may become a dominant seventh by changing the augmented sixth to a minor seventh enharmonically. It should also be recalled that ChII7 and Ch17 are exactly the same in design as V7. This suggests the formula: Since ChII7 and ChI7 and V7 are similar in construction they are interchangeable in different keys: V7 of C may become ChII7 in F, or ChI7 in G.

98

Since a German sixth may become a V7 by enharmonic change, it may also become ChII7 or ChI7. Therefore the following is possible:

Ex. 181

From the above it will be seen that modulation may be made between certain keys by using the Gn6 of the new key, if it is V7, ChII7 or ChI7 in the original key:

Ex. 182

The diminished seventh on the raised subdominant is frequently used enharmonically. Since all diminished sevenths are similar in construction, and since there are three diminished sevenths in every key, therefore one may assume the function of the other, that is xIV7o may become VII7o in another key, and III7o in another. It should be remembered that diminished sevenths are derivatives of primary ninths and occur on VII, xIV and III. The following shows a diminished seventh with its three functions:

Ex. 183

In using the diminished seventh chord in enharmonic modulation, it should always occur on the raised subdominant of the new key.

99

Ex. 184

B♭—   to   C+

The above is not a chromatic modulation properly speaking, since
the diminished seventh is a diatonic chord on VII in the first key,
which is minor.

5. *Additional suggestions.* Having discussed the several forms of
modulation, it should be left to the student to use the type of
modulation he feels to be best. There are always smooth modulations
available, no matter how remote the key.

Since the pivot chord is the only variable feature in modulation,
a list of pivot chords for any type of modulation is here given:

(a) Modulation to related keys:

Use the first available chord in the new key from these: II, IV,
VI, Ib.

(b) Modulation to keys a major or minor third apart (such as
C to A, C to A♭, C to E, C to E♭) Use the minor triad on IV of
the sharper key, that is, the key whose signature has the greater
number of sharps or the lesser number of flats.

(c) Modulation to other keys:

Use the first available chord in the new key from these: Gn6,
N6, xIV7o.

The first two of the above may be difficult to approach, so, in
case of such difficulty, the last chord listed always makes a good
modulation.

(d) Transition to any key: proceed at once to the new V7.

If this chord does not make a chromatic change, insert IV or V
of the first key.

EXERCISES

Aim for *neatness* and *accuracy.*

1. Modulate gradually, using not more than five chords, with
some passing notes and suspensions between these keys:

A + to D+ ; B + to F ♯+ ; C ♯+ to A ♯— ; D + to F ♯— ;
F + to G— ; E — to G+ ; F — to C —; D — to G—; B ♭— to
A ♭+ ; G — to E ♭+ .
E + to G + ; F+ to A ♭+ ; B + to G+ ; A+ to F + ; E ♭+ to
C + ; A ♭+ to C + ; B+ to D+ .

2. Modulate as smoothly as possible between these keys, using chromatic or enharmonic movement when effective:

A + to B ♭+ ; E + to E ♭+ ; B + to C ♯+ ; B − to A − ; C− to E ♭− ; A + to F − ; D + to B ♭− ; D♯− to E + : B ♭− to F + ; E + to A ♭+ ; D ♭+ to E + ;A ♭− to B − ; C − to G ♯− ; D ♭+ to A + .

3. Add three parts above the following figured basses:

4. Harmonize the following melodies:

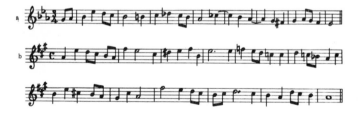

CHAPTER XX

HARMONIZATION OF BASSES

1. *Pedal basses.* A pedal bass, or pedal, or pedal point (all of these terms are in common use), is a bass note held or repeated during three or more changes of harmony above it. Sometimes such a note is placed in another part and is then known as an inverted pedal.

The only notes which are of any value as pedal notes are the dominant and the tonic.

(a) Tonic pedal. The harmony used when the tonic pedal commences must contain such note as a concord, therefore the chord must be I, VI or IV. Any harmony in reason may be used above the pedal after the first chord, provided the pedal ends as part of the harmony — if the final chord contains the tonic as a discord, it is obvious that it must resolve correctly.

When a tonic pedal is used at the beginning of a phrase, diatonic harmony with some passing notes is best above it. If it occurs at the end of the last phrase, forming an extension (sometimes known as a codetta) it is better to use a modulation to the subdominant above it:

Ex. 185

(b) Dominant pedal. This is generally found in the few bars preceding the final cadence, and it is sometimes followed by a tonic pedal. It is treated in the same way as a tonic pedal, in that it must begin and end as part of the harmony. Between these two points, and if the pedal is long enough, almost any modulation is good above the bass, particularly that to the supertonic minor (if the music is in a major key). When a pedal note is being used in the bass, the tenor

102

is the lowest moving part, and must be treated as a temporary bass of three part harmony. Here is a dominant pedal followed by a tonic pedal, both of which have modulations above them:

Ex. 186

If a pedal note is used in the soprano, care should be taken that harsh combinations do not occur. Dominant harmony should not be written below the tonic pedal, because the leading note always sounds harsh when it is below the tonic.

2. *Unfigured basses.* If the student has been very careful in his study of figured basses, he will have noticed certain features that are almost constantly found: sharp notes rising; flat notes falling; leaps of a fourth or fifth very frequently used; notes tied or repeated over a bar line which fall rather than rise. All such moving notes are easy to manage when the figures are given, but when there are no figures, the student is sometimes at a loss to know which chords are best to use. The figuring of basses involving modulation was discussed in Chapter XIII but some additional general rules may be of help now that the student has a better technique at his command:

(a) When a bass begins with a long note tied over the bar and falling one step, the note which is to fall should be harmonized just before it falls either as a suspension or as a third inversion of a chord of the seventh:

Ex. 187

(b) When a long note occurs anywhere, the upper parts should have some movement. If the note is very long it should be treated as a pedal (usually a dominant pedal). If it lasts for only one bar, movement may be made above it by changing the upper parts to other positions of the same chord and adding passing notes:

Ex. 188

(c) If the bass moves about quickly, the upper parts should not have too many notes, and certainly not too many changes of chord. Some of the bass notes should be treated as unessentials.

Ex. 189

(d) If a bass becomes syncopated, the chords should change on the strong beats (first and third beats in common time). As a general rule there should be one change of harmony inside each bar — on the third beat in both 3/4 and 4/4 time:

Ex. 190

(e) Modulations should be definitely determined before the plan of the whole is decided. At the half way resting place there is usually a modulation to the dominant. Preceding this modulation there may be a short transition or modulation to other related keys on the sharp (or dominant) side of the original key — in C + these are A − and E −. After the middle cadence an extraneous modulation is good, then a move to the subdominant or its relative minor. The student is advised not to move out of the key too soon. After the key has been firmly established, modulations may occur in quick succession, although sufficient time must be allowed to re-establish the key at the end. Here is a bass with the keys through which it passes is indicated.

Ex. 191

(f) If the bass is at all agitated, it is better to let the melody move by contrary motion. It is not necessary to move all the parts at once. Rests give character to the music; so do suspensions and passing notes. When the bass leaps from a very short note, that note should be harmonized, as it is part of the chord, and the preceding note is invariably an unessential note:

Ex. 192

3. *Ground basses.* A ground bass is a musical idea presented in the bass and repeated several times with different harmony used in each repetition. If a complete composition is thus made, with about twenty statements of the bass, such a work is known as a passacaglia. The student will probably find his ingenuity exhausted in three or four repetitions.

There must be no seams between the statements of the theme; in other words, cadential figures must not be conclusive at these points but lead into something more interesting as the music progresses. Here is a suggested plan for writing three presentations of a ground bass:

(a) First statement: Two part harmony, using either a soprano or a tenor above the given bass. If a soprano is used it should not be too high. The harmony suggested by each accented note should be simple. The rhythm of the melody should be in contrast to that of the bass, and should have good melodic design, accomplished by a few unessential notes. The melody may start after a short rest if desired.

(b) Second statement: Use three part harmony, soprano and alto, or alto and tenor. Let the chords be simple but use two or three modulations to related keys if possible, with some suspensions and passing notes or appoggiaturas.

(c) Third statement: Four parts. This is the section for chromatic chords, which may be introduced in other keys as well as the main key. Sometimes the final cadence is extended by a tonic pedal, over which interesting upper parts should be added.

Ex. 193

EXERCISES

Aim for *neatness* and *accuracy*.

1. Harmonize the following unfigured basses.

2. Harmonize the following ground basses, adding successively one, two and three parts.

DATE DUE / DATE DE RETOUR

- MEMO -